Handy Virginia Genealogy Handbook

Gary L.Morris

DEDICATION

To everyone who has a love of family and wants to find more of them!

Notes

Table of Contents

ACKNOWLEDGMENTS

Special appreciation to every genealogical volunteer or researcher who has taken the time to uncover the treasured resources that help us to find our family members of the past.

Genealogical Research in Virginia

As the site of the first American colony, there is a wealth of genealogical records and resources available for tracing your family history in Virginia. Because of the abundance of information held at many different locations, tracking down the records for your ancestor can be an ominous task. Don't worry though, we know just where they are, and we'll show you which records you'll need, while helping you to understand:

- What they are

- Where to find them

- How to use them

These records can be found both online and off, so we'll introduce you to online websites, indexes and databases, as well as brick-and-mortar repositories and other institutions that will help with your research in Virginia. So that you will have a more comprehensive understanding of these records, we have provided a brief history of the "Old Dominion State" to illustrate what type of records may have been generated during specific time periods. That information will assist you in pinpointing times and locations on which to focus the search for your Virginia ancestors and their records.

A Brief History of Virginia

When the first English speaking peoples arrived early in the 17th century, Tidewater Virginia was populated mostly by Algonkian-speakers. The natives were hunters and fishers as well planters who lived in the pole-framed dwellings we know as teepees, which formed small, barricaded towns. The area around Piedmont was the home of the Monacan, Manahoac, and Tutelo, all of the Sioux family, while the Cherokee lived in the far southwestern triangle Virginia.

The first permanent English settlement, not only in Virginia, but what was to become America, was established at Jamestown on 13 May 1607. The new land was named Virginia in honor of her majesty Queen Elizabeth I, the "Virgin Queen." The London Company (also called the Virginia Company) sponsored the first successful settlement, a joint-stock venture chartered by King James I in 1606. The entire American coast between 30° and 45°N and extending inland for 50 mi (80 km) was designated as Virginia, the are was further extended in 1609 and again in 1612 to include the entire area from California to east of the Bermuda Islands.

The early settlers of Jamestown suffered internal strife, conflict with the Native Americans in the area, and starvation. They were at the point of deserting the colony when three supply ships arrived in the nick of time in 1610, one of them carrying a certain Capt. John Smith, whose military skill and resourcefulness would inevitably save the colony from extinction. Captain Smith is best known for his marriage to the Algonquian Princess, Pocahontas. Smith also charted the coast of Virginia and established the colonial tobacco industry.

King James I revoked the Virginia Company's charter in 1624, and the colon y would remain loyal to the crown until 1776. Despite hardships and setbacks such as disease and Indian attacks, Jamestown grew steadily, and soon the crown cast its eye towards taxation. After the general assembly attempted to collect taxes from an area that had no legislative representation in 1653, Colonel Thomas Johnson initiated the Northampton Declaration, which embodied the principle of "no taxation without representation." Thus the rallying cry for the American Revolution was born.

Following the Crown's inability to protect the Virginian settlers from Indian attacks, in 1676 the colonists sought their own security, finding it in a young planter by the name of Nathaniel Bacon. While fighting against the native forces, Bacon and his charges turned their fight against the Crown, sparking a short lived revolt which ended with Bacon's death from fever in October of the same year.

Material and cultural progress marked the end of the 17th century, and the capitol was moved from Jamestown to Williamsburg. Industry expanded beyond the production of tobacco, and immigrants from Germany, and Scotch-Irish flocked to the area. After the French and Indian War of 1756-63, Virginians lost confidence in the crown, though the war did give emergence to a young and talented Virginian militiaman by the name of George Washington.

Virginians repeatedly challenged actions by the crown after the French and Indian War, sometimes independently, other times joined by neighboring colonies. The Stamp Act was opposed in 1765, and Virginia joined Massachusetts in appealing to all other colonies to act against British governance. A boycott of British goods was initiated by Virginia in 1769, and joined the other colonies in Philadelphia for the First Continental Congress on 1774.

Virginia was the first of the colonies to instruct its delegates to vote for independence at the Continental Congress of 1776. It was a native Virginian, Thomas Jefferson who drafted the Declaration of Independence, and the same year the colony adopted their own constitution and declaration of rights, which became the basis for the Bill of Rights in the US Constitution. Virginians took the lead in the Revolutionary War, as Virginia was a major battlefield, and it was on Virginia soil that Cornwallis surrendered to now General George Washington at Yorktown on October 19, 1781.

Virginians occupied the presidency for all but four of the nation's first twenty eight years, George Washington of course being the first. The early part of the 19th century saw much concern over slavery, as the Virginian general assembly had consistently outlawed the importation of slaves from as early as 1700, only to be constantly overruled by the Crown. In 1778 the Virginia legislature, no longer subject to veto by the Crown, instructed that any slave brought into the state would be automatically freed upon arrival. The number of free blacks grew tenfold by 1810, and though some were able to support themselves as farmers and artisans, many could not find work.

Fearing that disillusioned and malcontent free blacks might incite rebellion in those who were still slaves, the general assembly decreed in 1806 that each slave emancipated must leave the state within one year or after reaching the age of 21. The slave revolt headed by Nat Turner in 1831 further increased white fears of black emancipation. Nevertheless, legislation to end slavery in Virginia failed adoption by only seven votes the following year.

Slavery was not the only issue faced by 19th century Virginians. The slavery Although the state become a leading center of artistic, scientific, and educational advancement, during this era, the Civil War brought such advances to a rapid end. The governor of Virginia at that time, Governor John Letcher was a Union man, as were the majority of the state's political leaders. Virginia only seceded from the Union after President Lincoln marched troops across the state to punish those that were in rebellion. Shortly thereafter, Richmond, Virginia's capitol since 1780, became the capitol of the Confederacy. As the principal battlefield of the Civil war, Virginia paid a heavy price during the conflict. The state was placed under military government in 1867, and though readmitted to the Union in 1870, was at that time a completely bankrupt state, with debt of over $45 million.

Important Virginia Battles

As a leader in the American Revolutionary War and the principal battlefield during the Civil War, there are many famous battles that have been fought in Virginia. Important Revolutionary War battles were fought at Great Bridge, Petersburg, and Yorktown, and Rootsweb has a complete listing of Virginia Civil War Battles.

The battle accounts that exist can be very effective in uncovering the military records of your ancestor. They can tell you what regiments fought in which battles, and often include the names and ranks of many officers and enlisted men.

Great Bridge, Petersburg, and Yorktown:
http://traveltips.usatoday.com/famous-revolutionary-war-battle-sites-virginia-3988.html

Virginia Civil War Battles:
http://freepages.military.rootsweb.ancestry.com/~posey1863/virginia_civil_war_battles.htm

Common Virginia Genealogical Issues and Resources to Overcome Them

Boundary Changes: Boundary changes are a common obstacle when researching Virginia ancestors. You could be searching for an ancestor's record in one county when in fact it is stored in a different one due to historical county boundary changes.

The **Atlas of Historical County Boundaries** can help you to overcome that problem. It provides a chronological listing of every boundary change that has occurred in the history of Virginia.

Atlas of Historical County Boundaries: http://publications.newberry.org/ahcbp/documents/VA_Consolidat ed_Chronology.htm#Consolidated_Chronology

Name Changes: Surname changes, variations, and misspellings can complicate genealogical research. It is important to check all spelling variations. Soundex, a program that indexes names by sound, is a useful first step, but you can't rely on it completely as some name variations result in different Soundex codes. The surnames could be different, but the first name may be different too. You can also find records filed under initials, middle names, and nicknames as well, so you will need to **get creative with surname variations** and spellings in order to cover all the possibilities. For help with surname variations read our instructional article on **How to Use Soundex**.

get creative with surname variations: http://obituarieshelp.org/blog/?p=634

How to Use Soundex: http://obituarieshelp.org/blog/?p=505

Virginia Genealogical Organizations and Archives

Genealogical resources include not only records, but the organizations that house them, or can direct you to them. These institutions include: Archives, Libraries, Genealogical Societies, Family History Centers, Universities, Churches, and Museums.

Following are links to their websites, their physical addresses, and a summary of the records you can find there.

<u>Archives and Libraries</u>

Virginia Historical Society (State Archives) – Manuscripts collection, African American history, Civil War material, indexes to all of the Virginia census records from 1810 to 1920, immigration and passenger ship records, Wills, Marriages, Births and Deaths, Bibles, Newspapers, Maps, and more.

428 North Boulevard
Richmond, Virginia 23220

Phone: (804) 358.4901

Virginia Historical Society: http://www.vahistorical.org/

The Library of Virginia - African American and Native American resources', Vital Records, Naturalization records, Military records, Newspapers and Magazines, Tax Records, Virginia Land Office Patents and Grants, Women's History

800 East Broad Street
Richmond, Virginia 23219-8000

Phone: (804) 692-3500

The Library of Virginia: http://www.lva.lib.va.us/

University of Virginia Library – Historical newspapers and periodicals, bibliographies, Census records, Family histories and Surname indexes

P.O. Box 400113
Charlottesville, Virginia 22904

University of Virginia Library:
http://www2.lib.virginia.edu/genealogy/general/libraryresources.html

John D. Rockefeller, Jr. Library - Specialized collections of books, manuscripts, images and databases, resources specific to political and economic life of the thirteen colonies and the new republic, African American studies, and historical preservation

Colonial Williamsburg Foundation
313 First Street
Williamsburg, Virginia 23185

John D. Rockefeller, Jr. Library:
http://research.history.org/jdrlibrary.cfm

Valentine Richmond History Center - Rare books, atlases, city directories, personal papers, ledgers, business records, architectural drawings and diaries, approximately 150 maps of Richmond and Henrico County, newspaper articles, periodicals and serials published in Richmond, historical photograph collection

1015 East Clay Street
Richmond, Virginia 23219

Valentine Richmond History Center:
http://www.richmondhistorycenter.com/collections

National Archives at Philadelphia - Historically significant records of the Federal Agencies and Courts, in Delaware, Maryland, Pennsylvania, Virginia and West Virginia, dating from 1789 to the present, includes: Census Records, Ship's Passenger Lists, Naturalization Records, Military Service Records

900 Market Street
Philadelphia, PA 19107-4292
Telephone: 215-606-0100
Fax: 215-606-0111
Email: Philadelphia.archives@nara.gov

National Archives at Philadelphia:
http://www.archives.gov/philadelphia/public/family-history.html

Genealogical and Historical Societies

Genealogical and historical societies have access to extensive catalogues of genealogical data. They are also able to offer expert guidance for genealogical researchers. Many members are professional genealogists who are most willing to share their expertise in finding ancestors.

Genealogical Research Institute of Virginia – Family histories, Surname lists, excellent collection of Virginia Genealogy tutorials and other resources, including their extremely informative publication GRIVA News and Notes

P.O. Box 29178
Richmond, VA 23242-0178
Email: mail@griva.org

Genealogical Research Institute of Virginia:
http://grivagenealogy.wordpress.com/

Virginia Genealogical Society - Abstracts of Virginia Land Patents and Grants, 1600's to 1776, Index to Virginia Estates, 1800-1865, The Magazine of Virginia Genealogy

1900 Byrd Avenue, Suite 104
Richmond, Virginia 23230-3033
Tel: (804) 285-8954

Virginia Genealogical Society: http://www.vgs.org/

Albemarle Charlottesville Historical Society - Manuscript and printed materials, pertaining to the history of Charlottesville and Albemarle County; historical programs, lectures, exhibitions, and other educational activities; Historical library containing over 4,000 books and bound periodicals, other serial publications, manuscripts, maps, pamphlets, and vertical/subject files relating to the history of the community, as well as a collection of over 60,000 photographic images

McIntire Building
200 Second St., NE
Charlottesville, VA 22902-5245
Office: (434) 296-1492

Albemarle Charlottesville Historical Society:
http://www.albemarlehistory.org/

Additional Virginia Genealogy Resources

Virginia Mailing Lists

Mailing lists are internet based facilities that use email to distribute a single message to all who subscribe to it. When information on a particular surname, new records, or any other important genealogy information related to the mailing list topic becomes available, the subscribers are alerted to it. Joining a mailing list is an excellent way to stay up to date on Virginia genealogy research topics. Rootsweb have an extensive listing of **Virginia Mailing Lists** on a variety of topics.

Virginia Mailing Lists:
http://lists.rootsweb.ancestry.com/index/usa/VA/misc.html

Virginia Message Boards

A message board is another internet based facility where people can post questions about a specific genealogy topic and have it answered by other genealogists. If you have questions about a surname, record type, or research topic, you can post your question and other researchers and genealogists will help you with the answer. Be sure to check back regularly, as the answers are not emailed to you. The **Rootsweb Message Boards** are completely free to use.

Rootsweb Message Boards:
http://boards.rootsweb.com/localities.northam.usa.states/mb.ashx

Virginia Newspapers and Periodicals

Many genealogy periodicals and historical newspapers contain reprinted copies of family genealogies, transcripts of family Bible records, information about local records and archives, census indexes, church records, queries, land records, obituaries, court records, cemetery records, and wills. The following sites have historical Virginia newspapers and periodicals that you can search online or on-site.

Virginia Historical Society (State Archives) – Variety of historical newspapers from Virginia and other colonial era cities such as Philadelphia and Boston

428 North Boulevard
Richmond, Virginia 23220

Phone: (804) 358.4901

Virginia Historical Society: http://www.vahistorical.org/

GenealogyBank.com – free searchable database of Virginia newspaper archives, 1736-1986

GenealogyBank.como:
http://www.genealogybank.com/gbnk/newspapers/explore/USA/Vi
rginia/

The Online Books Page – links to historical Virginia books and periodicals available for viewing online

The Online Books Page:
http://onlinebooks.library.upenn.edu/webbin/book/browse?type=su
bject&c=c&key-virginia

Library of Congress Digital Newspaper Directory – free searchable database of historical U.S. newspapers dating from 1690-present

Library of Congress Digital Newspaper Directory: http://chroniclingamerica.loc.gov/search/titles/

NewspaperArchive.com – largest online database of historical newspapers in the world.

NewspaperArchive.com: http://newspaperarchive.com/

Historical Virginia Maps and Gazetteers

Maps are an integral part of genealogical research. They help us to locate landmarks, towns, cities, parishes, states, provinces, waterways and roads and streets. They also help us to determine when and where boundary changes might have taken place, and give us a visualization of the area we're researching in.

For locating place names, a gazetteer is the best possible resource for any genealogist. Gazetteers are also sometimes called "place name dictionaries", and can help you to locate the area in which you need to conduct research. Below are links to the maps and gazetteers for research in Virginia.

Peabody GNIS Service – Virginia: http://peabody.research.yale.edu/cgi-bin/Query.GNIS?ST=Virginia&SU=1

Color Landform Atlas – Virginia: http://fermi.jhuapl.edu/states/va_0.html

1985 U.S. Atlas: http://www.livgenmi.com/1895/VA/

Virginia Hometown Locator: http://virginia.hometownlocator.com/

Virginia City Directories.

City directories are similar to telephone directories in that they list the residents of a particular area. The difference though is what is important to genealogists, and that is they pre-date telephone directories. You can find an ancestor's information such as their street address, place of employment, occupation, or the name of their spouse. A one-stop-shop for finding city directories in Virginia is the **Virginia Online Historical Directories** which contains a listing of every available online historical directory related to Virginia. Another useful site is **US City Directories** which identifies printed, microfilmed, and online Virginia directories and their repositories.

Virginia Online Historical Directorieso:
https://sites.google.com/site/onlinedirectorysite/Home/usa/va

US City Directories: http://www.uscitydirectories.com/sd.htm

The **Family History Library** has directories for:

Richmond City, 1819-1860, and 1866-1935, and Norfolk City 1801, 1806, 1851, 1859, 1860, 1866-1901, 1902-1923, and 1924-1935

Family History Library:
http://familysearch.org/learn/wiki/en/Family_History_Library

Virginia Genealogical Records

<u>Birth, Death, Marriage and Divorce Records</u> – Also known as vital records, birth, death, and marriage certificates are the most basic, yet most important records attached to your ancestor. The reason for their importance is that they not only place your ancestor in a specific place at a definite time, but potentially connect the individual to other relatives. Below is a list of repositories and websites where you can find Virginia vital records.

Virginia Department of Health - Birth records 100 years after the date of the event; death, marriage, and divorce records, 25 years after the event

Office of Vital Records
2001 Maywill Street
Richmond, Virginia 23230
Tel: 804-662-6200

Mailing address:

P. O. Box 1000
Richmond, Virginia 23218

Virginia Department of Health:
http://www.vdh.state.va.us/vital_records/

Virginia Historical Society (State Archives) – Various county Birth, death, and marriage records from 18th century to present.

428 North Boulevard
Richmond, Virginia 23220

Phone: (804) 358.4901

Virginia Historical Society: http://www.vahistorical.org/

The Library of Virginia - Microfilm copies of births (1853–1896), deaths (1853–1896, 1912–1939), and marriages (1853–1935), surviving marriage records prior to 1853

800 East Broad Street
Richmond, Virginia 23219-8000

Phone: (804) 692-3500

The Library of Virginia: http://www.lva.lib.va.us/

New England Historic Genealogical Society Library - Virginia Vital Records from 18th and 19th centuries plus many county and town level records for Virginia

99 Newbury Street
Boston, MA 02116-3007
Telephone: 617-226-1231

New England Historic Genealogical Society Library:
http://www.americanancestors.org/library/

Family Search has the following Vital Record indexes that can be searched online for free:

- **Virginia, Births and Christenings, 1853-1917**

- **Virginia, Deaths and Burials, 1853-1912**

- **Virginia, Marriages, 1785-1940**

- **Virginia, Orange County Marriage Records, 1757-1938**

- **Virginia, Surry County Marriage Records, 1735-1950**

Virginia, Births and Christenings, 1853-1917:
https://familysearch.org/search/collection/1708660

Virginia, Deaths and Burials, 1853-1912:
https://familysearch.org/search/collection/1708697

Virginia, Marriages, 1785-1940:
https://familysearch.org/search/collection/1708698

Virginia, Orange County Marriage Records, 1757-1938:
https://familysearch.org/search/collection/1883379

Virginia, Surry County Marriage Records, 1735-1950:
https://familysearch.org/search/collection/1468642

Census Records

Census records are among the most important genealogical documents for placing your ancestor in a particular place at a specific time. Like BDM records, they can also lead you to other ancestors, particularly those who were living under the authority of the head of household.

Virginia Historical Society - Indexes to all of the Virginia census records from 1810 to 1920

428 North Boulevard
Richmond, Virginia 23220

Phone: (804) 358.4901

Virginia Historical Society: http://www.vahistorical.org/

University of Virginia Library – Copies of original Federal Census books, 1790 - 1930

P.O. Box 400113
Charlottesville, Virginia 22904

University of Virginia Library:
http://www2.lib.virginia.edu/genealogy/general/libraryresources.html

National Archives at Philadelphia – Federal census records 1790 - 1930

900 Market Street
Philadelphia, PA 19107-4292
Telephone: 215 606-0100
Fax: 215-606-0111
Email: Philadelphia.archives@nara.gov

National Archives at Philadelphia:
http://www.archives.gov/philadelphia/public/family-history.html

New England Historic Genealogical Society Library -
Miscellaneous Virginia Censuses and Substitutes: 1788-1822, 1840

99 Newbury Street
Boston, MA 02116-3007
Telephone: 617-226-1231

New England Historic Genealogical Society Library:
http://www.americanancestors.org/library/

The **Free Census Project** has transcribed many Virginia indexes and new material is added daily

Free Census Project: http://usgwcensus.org/cenfiles/va.htm

Access Genealogy – Virginia county census records dating from 1810-1930

Access Genealogy:
http://www.accessgenealogy.com/census/virginia-census-records.htm

African American Census Schedules Online – slave schedules, mortality schedules, slave-owners census

African American Census Schedules Online:
http://www.afrigeneas.com/aacensus/ga/

Native Americans in Census Records (US National Archives)

Native Americans in Census Records:
http://www.archives.gov/research/census/native-americans/

Virginia Church Records

Church and synagogue records are a valuable resource, especially for baptisms, marriages, and burials that took place before 1900. You will need to at least have an idea of your ancestor's religious denomination, and in most cases you will have to visit a brick and mortar establishment to view them.

Most church records are kept by the individual church, although in some denominations, records are placed in a regional archive or maintained at the diocesan level. Local Historical Societies are sometimes the repository for the state's older church records. Below are links archives that maintain church records, as well as a few databases that can be viewed online.

The **Family History Library** contains many church records from a variety of denominations on microfilm.

Family History Library:
http://familysearch.org/learn/wiki/en/Family_History_Library

Virginia Historical Society (State Archives) – Variety of church records dating from 17th to the 20th century. Denominations represented are Baptists, Catholics, Christian Church (Disciples of Christ), Episcopalians, Friends, Lutheran and German Reformed Church, Methodists, Presbyterians, and Unitarian-Universalists. Records include minute and vestry books, unpublished church histories, and parish registers. Also records from convents and church-supported homes for the aged in Richmond

428 North Boulevard
Richmond, Virginia 23220

Phone: (804) 358.4901

Virginia Historical Society: http://www.vahistorical.org/

Central Repositories for Denominational Records

<u>Church of Jesus Christ of Latter-day Saints (Mormons)</u>

Early Mormon Church records for Virginia can be found on film located at the LDS Family History Library in Salt Lake City and can be searched via the **Family History Library Catalog**

Family History Library Catalog:
https://familysearch.org/eng/Library/FHLC/frameset_fhlc.asp

The **Church History Library** has an even broader collection of historical church records than the Family History Library.

Church History Library

15 East North Temple
Salt Lake City, Utah 84150-1600
Phone: (801) 240-2272

Church History Library:
https://history.lds.org/?lang=eng#FlashPluginDetected

<u>Baptist</u>

Virginia Baptist Historical Society
Boatwright Memorial Library
28 Westhampton Way
University of Richmond, VA 23173
Telephone: (804)289-8669

Virginia Baptist Historical Societyo:
http://www.baptistheritage.org/

American Baptist Historical Society
1106 South Goodman Street
Rochester, NY 14620
Phone: (716) 473-1740

American Baptist Historical Society: http://abhsarchives.org/

Congregational

Congregational Library
14 Beacon Street
Boston, MA 02108
Phone: (617) 523-0470
Fax: (617) 523-0470

Congregational Library http://www.14beacon.org/

Presbyterian

Presbyterian Church Archives
Union Presbyterian Seminary in Virginia
3401 Brook Road
Richmond, VA 23227
Telephone: (800)229-2990 or (804)355-0671
Fax :(804)355-3919

Presbyterian Church Archives: http://www.upsem.edu/

Presbyterian Historical Society
425 Lombard Street
Philadelphia, PA 19147
Telephone: 1-215-627-1852
Fax: 1-215-627-0509

Presbyterian Historical Society http://www.history.pcusa.org/

Methodist

McGraw-Page Library
Randolph Macon College
P.O. Box 5005
202 Henry Street
Ashland VA. 23005-5505
Tel: 804-752-7200

McGraw-Page Library:
http://library.rmc.edu/specialcollections/methdist.html

Episcopal

Episcopal Diocese of Virginia
110 West Franklin Street
Richmond, Virginia 23220-5095
Tel: 804.643.8451
Fax: 804.644.6928

Episcopal Diocese of Virginia:
http://regionone.thediocese.net/Churches_in_Region_1/

Lutheran

Virginia Synod
220 College Lane
Salem, VA, 24153
Tel: 540-389-1000
Fax: 540-389-5962

Virginia Synod: http://www.vasynod.org/

Roman Catholic

Diocese of Richmond

7800 Carousel Lane
Richmond, VA 23294-4201
Tel: (804) 359-5661

Diocese of Richmond: http://www.richmonddiocese.org/

Diocese of Wilmington (DE)

8 Old Church Road,
Greenville DE 19807

Mailing Address:

PO Box 2030
Wilmington DE 19899
Telephone: (302) 655-0597
E-mail: donndevine@aol.com

Diocese of Wilmington (DE): http://www.cdow.org/

Diocese of Arlington

200 North Glebe Road
Arlington, VA 22203
Tel: 703-841-2500
Toll Free: 1-800-963-2505
Email: communications@arlingtondiocese.org

Diocese of Arlington: http://www.arlingtondiocese.org/

Virginia Military Records

More than 40 million Americans have participated in some kind of war service since America was colonized. The chance of finding your ancestor amongst those records is exceptionally high. Military records can even reveal individuals who never actually served, such as those who registered for the two World Wars but were never called to duty.

Below are a number of links to websites and archives that contain Virginia military records.

The Library of Virginia - Records of the French and Indian War, the American Revolution, and the Civil War, as well as limited information about Virginia's participants in the War of 1812, World War I, and other wars. Includes: Virginia Soldiers of the American Revolution (1912–1913; Historical Register of Virginians in the Revolution: Soldiers, Sailors, Marines, 1775–1783; and Muster Rolls of the Virginia Militia in the War of 1812, and Civil War records of Officers and Enlisted Men
800 East Broad Street
Richmond, Virginia 23219-8000

Phone: (804) 692-3500

The Library of Virginia: http://www.lva.lib.va.us/

Virginia Historical Society (State Archives) – Civil War records, colonial militia

428 North Boulevard
Richmond, Virginia 23220

Phone: (804) 358.4901

Virginia Historical Society: http://www.vahistorical.org/

National Archives and Records Administration - World War I Draft Registration Cards, Microfilm Roll List

8601 Adelphi Road
College Park, MD 20740-6001
Toll free: 1-866-272-6272

National Archives and Records Administration:
http://www.archives.gov/research/military/ww1/draft-registration/virginia.html

US Department of Veterans Affairs Nationwide Gravesite Locator – includes information on veterans and their family members buried in veterans and military cemeteries having a government grave marker.

US Department of Veterans Affairs Nationwide Gravesite Locator: http://gravelocator.cem.va.gov/

Family Search has the following indexes which are searchable online for free:

- **Virginia, Civil War Service Records of Confederate Soldiers, 1861-1865**

- **Virginia, Civil War Service Records of Union Soldiers, 1861-1865**

Virginia, Civil War Service Records of Confederate Soldiers, 1861-1865: https://familysearch.org/search/collection/1932382

Virginia, Civil War Service Records of Union Soldiers, 1861-1865: https://familysearch.org/search/collection/1932427

You may also find your ancestor's military records in the following databases:

United States General Index to Pension Files, 1861-1934: https://familysearch.org/search/collection/1919699

United States Index to Service Records, War with Spain, 1898

United States Index to Service Records, War with Spain, 1898: https://familysearch.org/search/collection/1919583

United States Index to Indian Wars Pension Files, 1892-1926 – military pension records of soldiers who fought in the Indian Wars between 1817 and 1898

United States Index to Indian Wars Pension Files, 1892-1926: https://familysearch.org/search/collection/1979427

United States Registers of Enlistments in the U.S. Army, 1798-1914 - index of men who enlisted in the United States Army, 1798-1914.

United States Registers of Enlistments in the U.S. Army, 1798-1914: https://familysearch.org/search/collection/1880762

United States Mexican War Pension Index, 1887-1926 - index to Mexican War pension files for service between 1846 and 1848

United States Mexican War Pension Index, 1887-1926: https://familysearch.org/search/collection/1979390

Civil War Soldiers Service Records - Service records for both Union and Confederate soldiers indexed by soldier's name, rank, and unit.

Civil War Soldier Service Records: http://go.fold3.com/civilwar_records/

Virginia Cemetery Records

As convenient as it is to search cemetery records online, keep in mind that there are a few disadvantages over visiting a cemetery in person. They are:

- Tombstone information is not always accurately transcribed

- The arrangement of the graves in a cemetery can be crucial as family members are often buried next to each other or in the same grave. This arrangement is not always preserved in the alphabetical indexes that are found online.

With that information in mind, the following websites have databases that can be searched online for Virginia Cemetery records.

Virginia Tombstone Transcription Project - death and burial records

Virginia Tombstone Transcription Project:
http://usgwtombstones.org/virginia/virginia.html

Virginia, Danville City Cemetery Records, 1833-2006 - records for several cemeteries in Danville, Virginia

Virginia, Danville City Cemetery Records, 1833-2006:
https://familysearch.org/search/collection/1386587

African American Cemeteries Online – African American, slave, and Native American cemetery records

African American Cemeteries Online:
http://africanamericancemeteries.com/ar/

Access Genealogy – database of Virginia cemetery record transcriptions

Access Genealogy:
http://www.accessgenealogy.com/cemetery/virginia-cemetery-records.htm

Find a Grave – over 100 million grave records can be searched on this site. Search can be conducted by name, location, or cemetery name.

Find a Grave: http://www.findagrave.com/

Interment.net - A free online database containing approximately 4 million cemetery records from around the world.

Interment.net: http://www.interment.net/

Billion Graves – as the name imples, you can search a billion records including headstone photos, transcriptions, cemetery records, and grave locations.

Billion Graves:
http://billiongraves.com/pages/search/index.php#cemetery

Virginia Obituaries

Obituaries can reveal a wealth about our ancestor and other relatives. You can search our **Virginia Obituaries Listings** from hundreds of Virginia newspapers online for free.

Virginia Obituaries Listings:
http://obituarieshelp.org/virginia_newspaper_obituaries.html

Virginia Wills and Probate Records

The documents found in a probate packet may include a complete inventory of a person's estate, newspaper entries, witness testimony, a copy of a will, list of debtors and creditors, names of executors or trustees, names of heirs. They can not only tell you about the ancestor you're currently researching, but lead to other ancestors.

Virginia Historical Society (State Archives) – Wills, probates, family papers, estate records, inventories and court orders dating from mid 17th century

428 North Boulevard
Richmond, Virginia 23220

Phone: (804) 358.4901

Virginia Historical Society: http://www.vahistorical.org/

The Library of Virginia - Early County records containing wills, deeds, and court orders or minutes

800 East Broad Street
Richmond, Virginia 23219-8000

Phone: (804) 692-3500

The Library of Virginia: http://www.lva.lib.va.us/

Family Search has the following indexes that can be searched online for free:

- **Virginia, Isle of Wight County Records, 1634-1951**

Virginia, Isle of Wight County Records, 1634-1951:
https://familysearch.org/search/collection/2034267

Virginia Immigration and Naturalization Records

The naturalization process generated many types of records, including petitions, declarations of intention, and oaths of allegiance. These records can provide family historians with information such as a person's birth date and place of birth, immigration year, marital status, spouse information, occupation, witnesses' names and addresses, and more.

If your ancestor lived in or near a large city, or near a city where U.S. courts convened, you may find naturalization records in the **U.S. District Court** before 1906.**U.S. District Court**: http://www.uscourts.gov/FederalCourts/UnderstandingtheFederalCourts/DistrictCourts.aspx

For the rural areas of Virginia, naturalization records may be found with the **County Courts** in each county. Often the records were mixed in with other court proceedings making them difficult to locate. A few counties kept separate records for naturalization. After 1906, all naturalizations were handled in Federal District Courts.

County Courts: http://www.courts.state.va.us/directories/home.html

Virginia Historical Society (State Archives) – Large variety of immigration records and passenger lists dating from colonial era. One highlight is the record of the first settlers in the colonies of North America, 1654-1685, including the names with places of origin of more than 10,000 servants of foreign plantations who sailed from the port of Bristol to Virginia, Maryland, and other parts of the Atlantic coast, and also to the West Indies from 1654 to 1685

Virginia Historical Society: http://www.vahistorical.org/

The Library of Virginia - Virginia Naturalizations, 1657-1929

800 East Broad Street
Richmond, Virginia 23219-8000

Phone: (804) 692-3500

The Library of Virginia: http://www.lva.lib.va.us/

National Archives at Philadelphia - Microfilm of ship's
passenger lists for Baltimore, MD: Indexes 1820-1952, Passenger
Lists 1820-1948, Philadelphia, PA: Indexes 1800-1948, Passenger
Lists 1800-1945, Atlantic and Gulf Ports (small ports): Index
1820-1874, Passenger Lists 1820-1873, New York (Ellis Island):
Index only 1897-1943, Galveston, TX: Indexes 1896-1951,
Passenger Lists 1896-1951, Providence, RI: Index only 1911-1954,
St. Albans, VT (Canadian entries): Indexes 1895-1952, Passenger
Lists 1929-1949

Naturalizations: Alexandria, 1909-1981; Norfolk, 1851-1992;
Richmond, 1870-1990 (with gaps); Abingdon, 1913-1949; Big
Stone Gap, 1914-1944; Charlottesville, 1910-1957; Danville,
1907-1966; and Roanoke 1906-1990.

900 Market Street
Philadelphia, PA 19107-4292
Telephone: 215-606-0100
Fax: 215-606-0111
Email: Philadelphia.archives@nara.gov

National Archives at Philadelphia:
http://www.archives.gov/philadelphia/public/family-history.html

US National Archives – Immigration records, Naturalization records, Ship's Passenger lists

The National Archives and Records Administration
8601 Adelphi Road
College Park, MD 20740-6001
Tel: 1-866-272-6272; 1-86-NARA-NARAS

US National Archives: http://www.archives.gov/research/guide-fed-records/groups/085.html

Family Search has the following indexes which can be searched online for free:

- **Virginia, Naturalization Petitions, 1906-1929**

Virginia, Naturalization Petitions, 1906-1929:
https://familysearch.org/search/collection/1877093

Virginia Native American Records

The Library of Virginia - Native Americans in state records, county records, local records, school records, court records, personal papers, and church records

800 East Broad Street
Richmond, Virginia 23219-8000
Phone: (804) 692-3500

The Library of Virginia: http://www.lva.lib.va.us/

National Archives and Records Administration - Dawes Commission Final Cards of the Five Civilized Tribes

8601 Adelphi Road
College Park, MD 20740-6001
Toll free: 1-866-272-6272

National Archives and Records Administration:
http://www.archives.gov/research/military/ww1/draft-registration/virginia.html

Access Genealogy – Virginia Native American census records, tribal histories, and much more

Access Genealogy:
http://www.accessgenealogy.com/native/virginia-indian-tribes.htm

U.S. National Archives - information on American Indians who maintained their ties to Federally-recognized Tribes (1830-1970).

U.S. National Archives: http://www.archives.gov/research/native-americans/

Records of the Bureau of Indian Affairs (BIA)

Records of the Bureau of Indian Affairs (BIA):
http://www.archives.gov/research/guide-fed-records/groups/075.html

American Indians Records Repository - records dating from the 1700s including trust, education and other historic Indian Affairs records

American Indian Records Repository
Meritex Enterprises
17501 West 98th Street
Lenexa, KS 66219
Phone: 913-888-0601

American Indians Records Repository:
http://www.doi.gov/ost/records_mgmt/american-indian-records-repository.cfm

Missing Matriarchs – Resources for Researching Female Virginia Ancestors

Looking for female ancestors requires an adjustment of how we view traditional records sources. A woman's identity was often under that of her husband, and often individual records for them can be difficult to locate. The following resources are effective in locating female ancestors in Virginia where traditional records may not reveal them.

Bibliographies

- The Old Dominion in the Seventeenth Century: A Documentary History of Virginia, 1606-1689, Warren M. Billings (University of North Carolina Press, 1975)

- Good Wives, Nasty Wenches, and Anxious Patriarchs: Gender, Race, and Power in Colonial Virginia, Kathleen M. Brown University of North Carolina Press, 1996)

- First Flowerings: Early Virginia Quilts, DAR Museum, 1987

- Ladies of Richmond, the Confederate Capital, Katherine Jones (Bobbs-Merrill, 1961)

- The Free Women of St. Petersburg: Status and Culture in a Southern Town, 1784-1860, Suzanne Lebsock (Norton & Co., 1984)

- Virginians at Home: Family Life in the Eighteenth Century, Edward S. Morgan (Colonial Williamsburg Foundation, 1952)

- Virginia Women: The First Two Hundred Years, Suzanne Lebsock and Suzanne Smith Ray (Colonial Williamsburg Foundation, 1988)

Selected Resources for Virginia Women's History

Library of Virginia
800 East Broad Street
Richmond, Virginia 23219-8000

Fishburn Library
Hollins College
Hollins, VA 24020

Judy Mann DiStefano Women's History Collection
Annandale Campus Library
Northern Virginia Community College
8333 Little River Turnpike
Annandale, VA 22003

Ladies Association of the Union Archives
Mount Vernon
Mount Vernon, VA 22121

United Daughters of the Confederacy
328 North Boulevard
Richmond, VA 23211-0311

Common Virginia Surnames

The following surnames are among the most common in Virginia and are also being currently researched by other genealogists. If you find your surname here, there is a chance that some research has already been performed on your ancestor.

Adams, Addington, Agee, Alderson, Allen, Alley, Anderson, Arnold, Ash, Ashworth, Austin, Aytes, Babb, Baker, Baldwin, Ball, Barker, Barnett, Barrett, Bays, Beddo, Begley, Bellamy, Benton, Bickman, Bishop, Bledsaw, Bledsoe, Blessing, Bloomer, Boggs, Bolin, Booher, Booker, Booth, Bowen, Bowens, Brannon, Brickey, Brickley, Broadwater, Brotherton, Bruner, Bryant, Buckner, Burchette, Burns, Butler, Byrd, Cadrey, Cain, Caldwell, Campbell, Carbaugh, Carr, Carter, Castle, Cecil, Chance, Chasteen, Chess, Childress, Clark, Clendenin, Clendening, Cock, Cocke, Coley, Collins, Combs, Compton, Cowden, Cox, Craft, Craiger, Crawford, Creech, Cress, Crook, Cross, Crosse, Culbertson, Darnell, Darter, Daugherty, Davidson, Davis, Day, Dean, Dickenson, Dillon, Dingus, Dockery, Donaldson, Dooley, Dorton, Dougherty, Drape, Duffield, Dulaney, Duncan, Dungannon , Edens, Egan, Egans, Elam, Ernest, Estep, Estill, Evans, Ewing, Falin, Fields, Finch, Flanary, Flanery, Flannery, Fleenor, Ford, Fraley, Francisco, Franklin, Frazer, Frazier, Frederick, Fugate, Fulk, Fuller, Gadrey, George, Gibson, Gillam, Gilliam, Gilreath, Glass, Gobble, Godsey, Goode, Graham, Gray, Greear, Green, Greens, Greer, Grey, Griffin, Gulley, Hackney, Hagen, Haggy, Hagy, Hale, Hall, Hallix, Hamilton, Hamminds, Hammond, Hammonds, Hanchelle, Hardin, Harrell, Harrion, Harris, Hartsock, Hawkins, Haynes, Hays, Head, Henry, Hensley, Heron, Herren, Herron, Hickam, Hicks, Hill, Hillman, Hobbs, Honeycutt, Hood, Hopkins, Horn, Horton, Houseman, Howington, Huff, Humes, Hutchins, Hutchinson, Insinger, Isaac, Isaacs, Jenkins, Jennings, Jett, Johnson, Johnston, Jones, Kane, Kellion,

Ketron, Kilgore, Killion, Kindle, Lane, Large, Larkey, Larkins,
Lawson, Lea, Lewis, Lovell, Lucas, Lyons, Maddox, Maddux,
Malicoat, Mann, Marcum, Marrs, Mason, Matticks, Mayo,
McClure, McCracken, McDavid, McGuire, McMullin, McMurry,
McNew, McNutt, Mendenhall, Merritt, Miller, Montieth, Moore,
Morell, Morrison, Moseley, Moss, Mullings, Mullins, Myers, Neal,
Neeley, Neely, Neil, Neill, Nelson, Newberry, Nickels, Niel, Niell,
Orr, Osborn, Osborne, Owens, Page, Pannell, Patterson, Payne,
Pendleton, Pennington, Persinger, Peters, Pierce, Pierson, Poston,
Powers, Presely, Presley, Price, Purcell, Qualls, Quillin, Rainey,
Ramey, Ratliff, Reasor, Reed, Reeve, Renfroe, Rhodes, Rhoten,
Rhoton, Richards, Richmond, Riley, Roach, Robbins, Roberts,
Robinette, Robinson, Roe, Roller, Rose, Ruth, Salling, Salyers,
Sauders, Scalf, School, Scott, Shepard, Shoemaker, Shorte, Slagle,
Sloan, Sluss, Smith, Snodgrass, Southers, Spear, Spears, Speer,
Sprinkle, Sproles, Stacy, Stallard, Stanly, Stapleton, Starnes,
Stephenson, Stewart, Stinson, Stone, Sturgill, Sulfridge, Sullivan,
Tarter, Tate, Taylor, Templeton, Thomas, Thompson, Tipton,
Tomlinson, Treadway, Tredaway, Tredway, Twoer, VanNess,
Vansant, Vanzant, Vickers, Vinyards, Wade, Walker, Wallen,
Waters, Webb, Wells, White, Williams, Willis, Wilson, Wininger,
Wolf, Wolfe, Wood, Wright, Yost

ABOUT THE AUTHOR

Gary L. Morris worked from 2009 to 2014 as a professional researcher for a major player in the genealogy field. After tracing his family lineage back to 1683, he has decided to publish these helpful guides to share the valuable information he has discovered during his career to help others trace their family lineages. An avid genealogist himself, he hopes you will find this guide factual, thorough, helpful, and most of all, effective in helping you to find your family members.

www.ingramcontent.com/pod-product-compliance
Lightning Source LLC
Chambersburg PA
CBHW071138280526
45787CB00003B/1325